Silly Signs

Published and distributed by
TOBAR LIMITED
St. Margaret, Harleston, Norfolk, IP20 0TB, UK
www.tobar.co.uk

This edition printed in 2005

Printed in Poland

ISBN 1 903230 17 9

Silly Signs covers a wide range of mistakes and mistranslations. Gathered together here are some of the best examples of what happens when not enough thought goes into a sign or a warning label.

Sometimes it is because of an amusing error in translation, or sometimes it is because the full stop is in the wrong place. More often than not, though, it is the double entendres that are guaranteed to raise a giggle.

Weird and wonderful warnings are also always good for a laugh. Whether they are stating the downright obvious, or telling you not to do something that you would never even consider, they always raise the question: Are they warning us not to do this because someone has actually done it? If so, who?

The stupid signs collected here range from the best of British to American classics, taking in examples from Egypt, Switzerland and Australia en route. It is important to remember that, ridiculous though they may seem, these are all genuine signs, notices or warnings. And it's always worth keeping your eyes peeled – there are bound to be plenty more out there.

Eat here
and
get gas

At restaurant-petrol stations
throughout the USA

*We buy junk
and sell
antiques*

Outside a country shop

WE CLEAN ON THE SPOT

Outside a South London dry cleaners

No children allowed

In a maternity ward, Florida

**Warning:
Contains nuts**

On a peanut packet

**DO NOT
IRON
CLOTHES
ON BODY**

On packaging for an iron

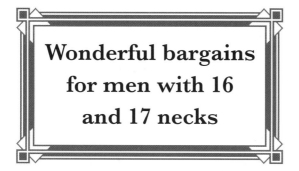

Wonderful bargains for men with 16 and 17 necks

Inside a clothing store

Take Notice:
When this sign
is under water
the road is
impassable

On a US highway

A safari park notice

In a London office block

DRIVE CAREFULLY WE HAVE TWO CEMETERIES AND NO HOSPITAL

A road sign, Branxton, USA

Those who throw objects at the crocodiles will be asked to retrieve them

A zoo sign

Attention Dog Guardians:
Pick up after your dogs.
Thank you
Attention Dogs:
Grrrrr, bark, woof.
Good dog

A park notice, Canada

PETS
FISH
REPTILES
SMALL ANIMALS
SENIOR CITIZENS
DISCOUNTS
HOME DELIVERY

In a pet shop's window

Welcome to our ool (notice there's no 'p' in it – let's keep it that way!)

Swimming pool warning

Our public bar is presently not open because it is closed. Manager

A sign outside a bar

Welcome to
Glendambo
Elevation: 150m
Population – Sheep: 22,500
Flies: 2,000,000
Humans: 30

A road sign, Glendambo USA

The town hall is closed until opening. It will remain closed after being opened.

A sign outside a UK town hall

PLEASE LEAVE YOUR VALUES AT THE FRONT DESK

In a hotel elevator, Paris

Special today - no ice cream

In a mountain inn, Switzerland

Please be safe. Do not stand, sit, climb or lean on zoo fences. If you fall, animals could eat you and that might make them sick. Thank you

At a zoo, Knoxville, USA

LADIES
LEAVE
YOUR CLOTHES HERE AND
SPEND THE AFTERNOON
HAVING A
GOOD TIME

In a launderette, Rome

Do not activate with wet hands

On an automatic hand-dryer

Caution! Cape does not enable user to fly

Warning on a child's Batman costume

Do not drive a car or operate machinery after taking this medication

Packaging for children's cough syrup

Not to be used as protection from a tornado

On a blanket from Taiwan

Instructions for a toaster

Warning:
Keep out of children

Instructions for Korean-made kitchen knife

DO NOT USE WHILE SLEEPING

Instructions on a hairdryer

Alligator
feeding Sunday
at 3pm
Bring the kids

A zoo sign

For same day service please give 24 hours notice

A launderette sign

After tea break staff should empty the teapot and stand upside down on the draining board

An office kitchen, London

Automatic washing machines. Please remove all your clothes when the light goes out

A launderette sign

OPEN SEVEN DAYS A WEEK AND WEEKENDS

A sign in a restaurant

Curl up
'n' dye
hair
salon

A hairdresser's sign

To aid your
enjoyment
please
eliminate dogs
and litter

A park notice

Be careful!
Goats like to
nibble on your
clothes and
butt

A petting zoo sign

Caution!
Water on
road during
rain

A road sign, USA

Give blood –
8 billion
mosquitoes
can't be wrong

A hospital sign, USA

Any persons (except players)
caught collecting golf balls on
this course will be prosecuted
and have their balls removed

A sign on a golf course

WE ALMOST NEVER CLOSE

A sign on a long-abandoned market site

Cattle please close gate

Sign outside a farm

Remove clothing
before
distributing in
washing machine

On a washing powder packet

Warning:
Remove
child before
folding

Warning on a pushchair

Same day dry cleaning All garments ready in 24 hours

A dry cleaner's notice

A sports jacket may be worn to dinner, but not trousers

In a hotel, USA

DO NOT USE ON FOOD

Notice on dishwasher liquid packaging

If you require room service, please open door and shout, 'room service!!'

In a hotel, Egypt

Do not spray in your face

Warning on a bottle of spray paint

Kids eat free
live clown
every Tuesday

A restaurant sign

FOR SERIOUS INJURIES, SEEK MEDICAL ATTENTION

Instructions on a box of plasters

Instructions
Open
packet.
Eat
nuts

On a packet of peanuts

**Warning:
Can become
hot in use**

Instructions on an iron

**CAUTION
NO
WARNING
SIGNS**

A road sign

**CAUTION!
Do NOT swallow
nails! May cause
irritation!**

On a box of household nails

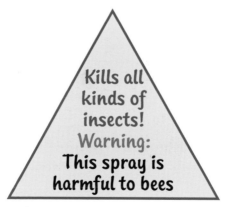

Kills all
kinds of
insects!
Warning:
**This spray is
harmful to bees**

Warning on a can of insect spray

Remove
lock
before
driving

Warning on a steering lock

This product contains
granules under
3 millimeters. Not
suitable for children
under the age of
14 years in Europe or
8 years in the USA

Warning on a packet of juggling balls

BEWARE OF BEING SWALLOWED BY CHILD DUE TO SMALL PARTS

Instructions on a toy made in China

Please do not wash hair or clothes in toilet

Rules in Japanese hotel bathroom

For indoor or outdoor use only

Warning on Christmas lights

Serving suggestion: Defrost

On a frozen dinner

**CAUTION:
AVOID DROPPING AIR
CONDITIONERS OUT
OF WINDOWS**

Warning on air conditioner

KEEP
AWAY FROM
CHILDREN

Label on bottle of baby lotion

These ear plugs are non toxic, but may interfere with breathing if caught in windpipe

Warning on ear plugs

IF SWALLOWED, PROMPTLY SEE DOCTOR

Warning on 4-pack of batteries

Made in America. Parts from Japan. Assembled in Mexico

On a guitar

SOME ASSEMBLY REQUIRED

Instructions on a 500-piece jigsaw puzzle

NOW HIRING BURGER AND FRIES

Fast food restaurant sign

Safe to use around pets and children, although it is not recommended that either be permitted to drink from toilet

Warning on toilet cleaner

Warning on an aspirin packet

Warning on sleeping tablets

If tunnel
is dark,
remove
sunglasses

Sign in a National Park, Tennessee

Emergency
telephone
174km ahead

Road sign, USA

Hot coffee can be DANGEROUS

Warning on a coffee cup

Explosives prohibited in the tunnel

Road sign, USA

Park sign, USA

Toilet sign, USA

Runaway vehicles only/ Emergency escape ramp

Road sign, Hawaii

Caution: Automatic Door (push to operate)

Sign on an office building

If you
don't see what
you're looking for
you've come to the
right place

Sign in an optometrist's office

**Waitresses
required for
breakfast**

In a café window

Customers who find our waiting staff rude should see the manager

A restaurant notice

No walking, sitting or playing on the grass in this pleasure park

London park rules

Due to increasing problems with litter louts and vandals we must ask anyone with relatives buried in the graveyard to do their best to keep them in order

A notice sent to residents of a UK parish

DO NOT PUT WET CLOTHES IN DRYERS, AS THIS CAN CAUSE IRREPARABLE DAMAGE

In a laundry room

TATTOOS
DONE
WHILE
YOU WAIT

Tattoo parlour sign

Hot beer,
lousy food,
bad service.
Welcome.
Have a nice day

A diner sign, USA

Road sign, USA

A road sign, UK

Soccer not allowed. Soccer may only be played in archery range

A park sign

Warning to young ladies – if you wear loose clothes, beware of the machinery. If you wear tight clothes, beware of the machinist

Notice in a clothes factory

For anyone who has children and doesn't know it, there is day care on the first floor

Sign in a hotel

A tailors, Hong Kong

Visitors are expected to complain at the office between the hours of 9 and 11 daily

Sign in a hotel, Greece

Good clean dancing every night but Sunday

Dance hall sign, USA

You are
invited to take
advantage
of the
chambermaid

Sign in a hotel, Japan

It is strictly forbidden on our Black
Forest camping site that people of
different sex, for instance, men and
women, live together in one tent
unless they are married with each
other for that purpose

Sign in the Black Forest, Germany

Notice: This package contains unassembled furniture and must be assembled prior to use. Assembly instructions enclosed

Label on a furniture kit

REMOVE THIS BEFORE DRIVING

Instructions for windscreen sunshield

Warning on a bottle of dog shampoo

On a can of pepper spray

Do not use for drying pets

Instructions for a microwave oven

Not to be used as a personal flotation device

Warning on an inflatable photo frame
measuring 6x10 inches

Sign in a train station, Hong Kong

Instructions on a shower cap

Shoes are required to eat in the canteen

Notice in a canteen

Large
women's
washroom,
third
floor

Sign in an office block, USA

The ladies of the church have cast off clothing of every kind and they may be seen in the church basement on Friday

Church jumble sale announcement

This being Easter Sunday, we will ask Mrs Lewis to come forward and lay an egg on the altar

Notice inside a church

Sign on a driveway

Road sign, India

Our wines leave you nothing to hope for

Sign in a Swiss restaurant

Please be quiet. We need to hear a pin drop

Sign in a bowling alley

Road sign, USA

Railway crossing sign, UK

English well
talking. Here
speeching
American

Shop sign, Majorca

Because of the impropriety
of entertaining guests of the
opposite sex in the bedroom,
it is suggested that the lobby
be used for this purpose

Sign in a hotel in Zurich

Do not use near open flame

Warning on a cigarette lighter

Please drive slowly and watch for old horses, blind dogs, unruly kids

Road sign, USA

Road sign, USA

This is not highway 89

Road sign, USA

Secret
wartime
tunnels.
No entry

Sign at entrance to tunnels, UK

Entrance only
Do not enter

Road sign, USA

Warning:
Unexploded
ordnance area.
Please stay within
picnic area.
Do not disturb
unidentified objects

Notice in a park

Instructions on a shampoo bottle

This camera
only works
when there is
film inside

Instructions on a camera

Do not operate
if the
appliance
stops working
entirely

Instructions for a grill

SECRET NUCLEAR BUNKER

Road sign, UK

Do not place your phone inside a microwave oven. This may damage the phone and the oven

Instructions for a mobile phone

Subway tunnel sign

Warning on hair colouring

Emergency stopping
only.
Whale watching is
NOT an emergency,
keep driving

Road sign, USA

A road sign

Drop your pants here and you will receive prompt attention

Sign outside a dry cleaners, USA

Our motto is to give our customers the lowest possible prices and workmanship

In a shop window, Maine, USA

Ask about our plans for owning your home

Sign at a loan company

Would the person who took the step ladder yesterday please bring it back or further steps will be taken

Sign in an office

Weekend giveaway/
Guaranteed
free child

Sign in a travel agents

NO SHIRT,
NO SHOES,
NO SERVICE

Notice in a café window, USA

For best results, start with clean bath tub before use

On a bottle of bath tub cleaner

ANTIQUE tables made here daily

A sign outside a furniture shop, USA

Billboard advert for a furniture store

An advert in a dentist's practice

A road sign, Australia

Please do not
spit too loud,
thank you

Sign in a train station, China